Texas History Bingo Book

COMPLETE BINGO GAME IN A BOOK

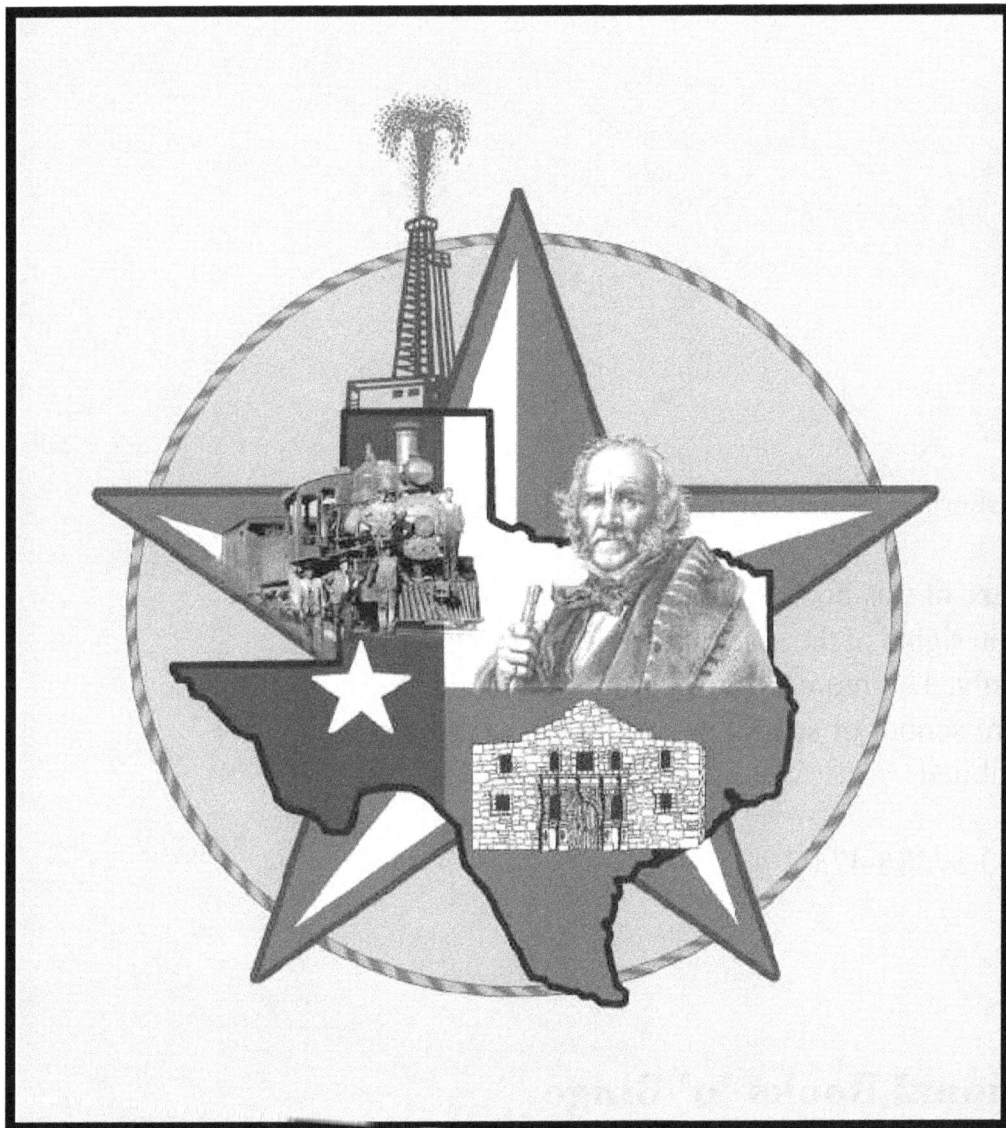

Written by Rebecca Stark

ISBN 978-0-87386-473-2

Educational Books 'n' Bingo

Printed in the U.S.A.

TEXAS HISTORY BINGO
Directions

INCLUDED:

List of Terms

Templates for Additional Terms and Clues

2 Clues per Term

30 Unique Bingo Cards

Markers

1. **Either cut apart the book or make copies of ALL the sheets. You might want to make an extra copy of the clue sheets to use for introduction and review. Keep the sheets in an envelope for easy reuse.**

2. Cut apart the call cards with terms and clues.

3. Pass out one bingo card per student. There are enough for a class of 30.

4. Pass out markers. You may cut apart the markers included in this book or use any other small items of your choice.

5. Decide whether or not you will require the entire card to be filled. Requiring the entire card to be filled provides a better review. However, if you have a short time to fill, you may prefer to have them do the just the border or some other format. Tell the class before you begin what is required.

6. There are 50 topics. Read the list before you begin. If there are any topics that have not been covered in class, you may want to read to the students the topic and clues before you begin.

7. There is a blank space in the middle of each card. You can instruct the students to use it as a free space or you can write in answers to cover topics not included. Of course, in this case you would create your own clues. (Templates provided.)

8. Shuffle the cards and place them in a pile. Two or three clues are provided for each topic. If you plan to play the game with the same group more than once, you might want to choose a different clue for each game. If not, you may choose to use more than one clue.

9. Be sure to keep the cards you have used for the present game in a separate pile. When a student calls, "Bingo," he or she will have to verify that the correct answers are on his or her card AND that the markers were placed in response to the proper questions. Pull out the cards that are on the student's card keeping them in the order they were used in the game. Read each clue as it was given and ask the student to identify the correct answer from his or her card.

10. If the student has the correct answers on the card AND has shown that they were marked in response to the *correct questions,* then that student is the winner and the game is over. If the student does not have the correct answers on the card OR he or she marked the answers in response to *the wrong questions,* then the game continues until there is a proper winner.

11. If you want to play again, reshuffle the cards and begin again.

Have fun!

TERMS INCLUDED

Alamo

Annexation

Aquifer(s)

Armadillo

Austin, TX

Stephen F. Austin

Barbed Wire

Borders

Jim Bowie

David G. Burnet

Caddo

Cattle

Comanche

Confederacy

Constitution

cotton

County (-ies)

Davy Crockett

Dallas

Declaration of Independence

Susanna Dickinson

El Paso

Empresario

Flag(s)

Goliad

Goodnight

Guadalupe

Houston, TX

Sam Houston

Juneteenth

Mirabeau B. Lamar

Lone Star

Missions

Sam Rayburn

Oil

Quanah Parker

Plains

President of the U.S.

Reconstruction

Republic of Texas

Rio Grande

San Antonio

Juan Seguín

Sheep

Tejanos

Texas Independence Day

Texas Rangers

Texas Revolution

William Travis

Treaty of Guadalupe Hidalgo

Additional Terms

Choose as many Texas History terms as you would like and write them in the squares. Repeat each as desired. Cut out the squares and randomly distribute them to the class. Instruct the students to place the square on the center space of their card.

Clues for Additional Terms

Write two or three clues for each of your Texas History terms.

<table>
<tr><td>

_____

1.

2.

3.

</td><td>

_____

1.

2.

3.

</td></tr>
<tr><td>

_____

1.

2.

3.

</td><td>

_____

1.

2.

3.

</td></tr>
<tr><td>

_____

1.

2.

3.

</td><td>

_____

1.

2.

3.

</td></tr>
</table>

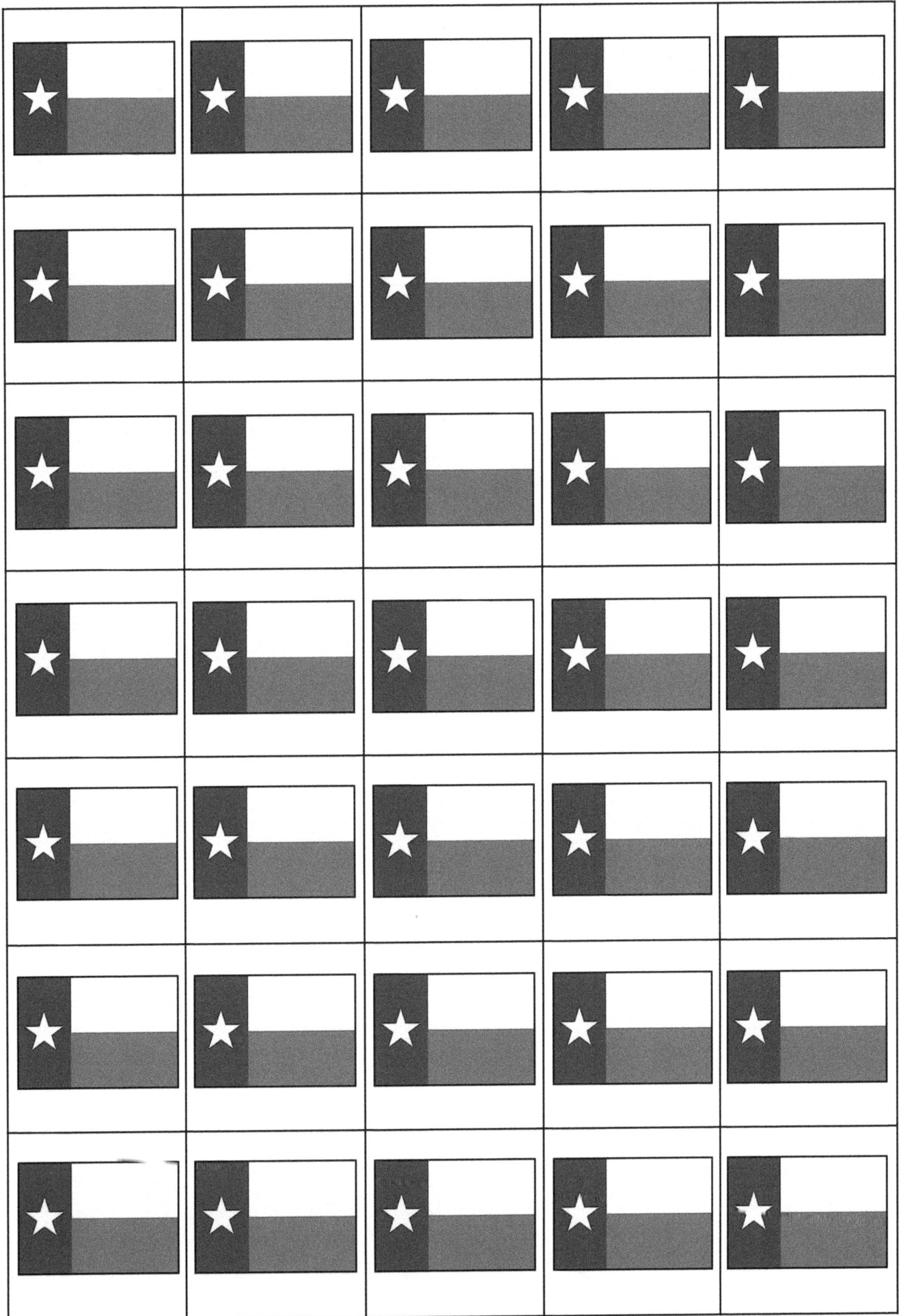

Alamo 1. Originally named Misión San Antonio de Valero, it was home to missionaries and Indian converts from 1724 to 1793. 2. It became the site of the most famous battle of the Texas Revolution. All 182 defenders of the ___ were killed.	**Annexation** 1. It is the act of incorporating a territory into a political unit such as a country. 2. ___ of Texas became official on December 29, 1845.
Aquifer(s) 1. The state depends upon ___, which are underground layers of earth or rock that yield water for wells and irrigation. 2. The Ogallala ___ is by far the most important in the state.	**Armadillo** 1. This small mammal has a leathery armor. 2. The nine-banded ___ is the only native species in the U.S. and is found in the south central part of the U.S., especially Texas.
Austin, TX 1. It is the capital of Texas. 2. It promotes itself as the Live Music Capital of the World.	**Stephen F. Austin** 1. He is known as the Father of Texas. The capital of Texas is named for him. 2. This empresario established a settlement on the banks of the Brazos River. It was the first Anglo settlement in Texas.
Barbed Wire 1. Before the invention of ___, livestock roamed freely. It was invented by Joseph Glidden in 1853. 2. The use of ___ to fence in land was the cause of many disagreements between ranchers and farmers.	**Borders** 1. The southern ___ of Texas are Mexico and the Gulf of Mexico. 2. Louisiana, Arkansas, Oklahoma, and New Mexico are all ___ of Texas.
Jim Bowie 1. As part of the Texian volunteer army, he took part in the Battle of Nacogdoches, the Battle of Conception and the Battle of the Alamo. 2. Like Davy Crockett and William Travis, ___ died defending the Alamo.	**David G. Burnet** 1. He was Interim President of the Republic of Texas. 2. He negotiated the Treaties of Velasco. Many Texians were angry that the treaty did not call for Santa Anna's execution.

Texas History Bingo

Caddo 1. The ___ were farmers in East Texas. The name "Texas" comes from a ___ word meaning "those who are friends." 2. The Tejas ___ lived near present-day Nacogdoches. The Kadohadacho ___ lived in villages along the Red River.	**Cattle** 1. Beef ___, especially longhorn, is the most important farm product of the state. 2. Drovers were cowboys who worked the ___ drives.
Comanche 1. The ___ were fierce warriors and great horsemen. During the mid to late 1800's they controlled a lot of land in Texas. 2. Quanah Parker was a ___ leader.	**Confederacy** 1. Texas became a member of the ___ after it seceded from the Union. 2. Edward Clark became governor of Texas when Governor Sam Houston refused to pledge allegiance to the ___.
Constitution 1. The state ___ of Texas has been in effect since 1876 although it has more than 450 amendments. 2. The main reason the Texas ___ has so many amendments is that the state only has those powers explicitly granted to it.	**Cotton** 1. ___ is the most important cash crop in Texas. 2. The state of Texas produces about 1/4 of the nation's ___. Only beef and nursery industries rank higher in cash receipts.
County (-ies) 1. There are 254 ___ in Texas. 2. Each ___ is divided into four precincts.	**Davy Crockett** 1. This hero of the Alamo had been known for his humorous tall tales. 2. Before going to Texas, he served in the Tennessee Legislature and in the U.S. Congress as a representative from Tennessee.
Dallas 1. The ___-Fort Worth metropolitan area is the fourth largest in the United States and the largest in Texas. 2. President John F. Kennedy was assassinated in this city.	**Declaration of Independence** 1. George C. Childress is credited with being the author of the Texas ___. 2. The Texas ___ was adopted by the Convention of 1836 on March 2, 1836, and formally signed the next day.

Texas History Bingo

Susanna Dickinson 1. She was the only adult Anglo survivor of the Battle of the Alamo. 2. Her husband was killed by the Mexican Army at the Battle of the Alamo.	**El Paso** 1. This city is on the Rio Grande. 2. This city is across the river from Ciudad Juárez in Mexico.
Empresario(s) 1. ___ were granted to right to settle on Mexican land in exchange for recruiting settlers and taking responsibility for them. 2. Stephen Austin was an ___. He founded San Felipe de Austin on the Banks of the Brazos River.	**Flag(s)** 1. Texas is only state to serve under 6 ___: Spain, France, Mexico, the Republic of Texas, the Confederacy and the United States. 2. The Texas ___ is red, white and blue. It is called the Lone Star ___.
Goliad 1. Like the defenders of the Alamo, the men who died at ___ served as martyrs to their cause. 2. James Fannin's troops were defeated at ___ and Fannin was executed. The event is known as the ___ Massacre.	**Goodnight** 1. Charles ___ founded the first ranch in the Texas Panhandle. He is called the Father of the Texas Panhandle. 2. In 1866 he and Oliver Loving drove a herd of cattle along what would later be known as the ___-Loving Trail.
Guadalupe 1. The ___ Mountains are in western Texas. 2. The highest point in Texas is ___ Peak. It has an elevation of 8,749 feet.	**Houston, TX** 1. NASA's Johnson Space Center is located in this city. 2. It is the largest city in Texas. It was incorporated in 1837 and named after the man who was at that time president of the Republic of Texas.
Sam Houston 1. He was the first and third president of the Republic of Texas. 2. He was the seventh governor of Texas but gave up governorship by refusing to pledge allegiance to the Confederacy.	**Juneteenth** 1. This holiday originated in Galveston. It is also known as Emancipation Day. 2. It became a legal state holiday in 1980. It celebrates the day on which abolition was announced in the state.

Texas History Bingo

Mirabeau B. Lamar 1. He is sometimes called the Father of Texas Education. 2. As president of the republic, ___ tried to drive out the Native Americans. This angered Sam Houston, who was president both before and after him.	**Lone Star** 1. Texas is nicknamed the ___ State. 2. Texas's flag is known as the ___ flag.
Missions 1. Spanish ___ were established to try to convert the Native Americans to Christianity. 2. There were a total of 26 ___ established in Texas. The first was San Francisco de la Espada.	**Sam Rayburn** 1. This Texas legislator was speaker of the House for many years. 2. At the time of his death in 1961 his 48 years of service in the House of Representatives was the longest ever recorded.
Oil 1. The first ___ field was drilled near the town of Nacogdoches in 1866. 2. The second ___ field, which was discovered at Corsicana, marked the start of the ___ boom in the state. A refinery was built there.	**Quanah Parker** 1. He was a great Comanche leader. 2. His mother, Cynthia Ann Parker, was a white woman who had been taken captive by the Comanche as a young girl.
Plains 1. The Central ___; Gulf Coastal ___; and High ___ , sometimes called Panhandle ___, are 3 geographic regions of Texas. 2. There are 4 main geographic regions of Texas: the 3 ___ regions and the Mountains and Basins.	**President of the United States** 1. Lyndon Baines Johnson was a Texan who became the 36th ___. 2. George H.W. Bush was a Texan who became the 41st ___. His son, George W., became the 43rd ___.
Reconstruction 1. This name is given to the period following the American Civil War. 2. During ___ Southerners tried to rebuild their economy and gain readmission to the United States.	**Republic of Texas** 1. Texas was called the ___ when it was a sovereign nation. 2. The ___ was in existence from 1836 to 1845.

Texas History Bingo

Rio Grande 1. This marks the boundary between Mexico and Texas. 2. It is called Rio Bravo in Mexico.	**San Antonio** 1. First-time visitors to ___ usually visit the Alamo. 2. This city is known for its River Walk.
Juan Seguín 1. He was a Tejano leader who fought on the side of the Texans against Santa Anna. 2. This Tejano was sent by Colonel Travis to cross enemy lines to try to get help for those at the Alamo.	**Sheep** 1. Cattlemen and farmers did not get along with the ___ ranchers. 2. Cattlemen and farmers were angered because ___ grazed the grass too short and trampled the crops.
Tejanos 1. They are Texans of Mexican descent. 2. Juan Seguín and other ___ revolted against the tyranny of Santa Anna.	**Texas Independence Day** 1. ___ is celebrated on March 2. 2. This holiday commemorates the adoption of the Texas Declaration of Independence.
(Texas) Rangers 1. The ___ were first used in 1823 by Stephen Austin to protect the settlements against Indian attacks. 2. Austin referred to them as ___ because they had to range over a large area.	**Texas Revolution** 1. This war was between Mexico and Texians, Anglo-American residents of Texas when Texas was part of Mexico. 2. It began with the Battle of Gonzales on October 2, 1835, and ended with the Battle of San Jacinto April 21, 1836.
William Travis 1. He was the Texan commander during the Siege and Battle of the Alamo. He was only 26 when he died there. 2. During the siege at the Alamo ___ wrote a letter appealing for reinforcements. Texas History Bingo	**Treaty of Guadalupe Hidalgo** 1. Under the terms of the ___, Mexico recognized the Rio Grande as the southern boundary of the United States. 2. The ___ ended the Mexican War As a result Mexico ceded all claims to Texas. © Barbara M. Peller

Texas History Bingo

Flag(s)	Susanna Dickinson	Juan Seguín	Texas Revolution	Tejanos
Jim Bowie	Alamo	(Texas) Rangers	Lone Star	Davy Crockett
Republic of Texas	Quanah Parker		Goodnight	Treaty of Guadalupe Hidalgo
William Travis	Annexation	Dallas	Guadelupe	Goliad
Cotton	Comanche	David G. Burnet	County(-ies)	Declaration of Independence

Texas History Bingo

William Travis	Rio Grande	Juneteenth	Sam Rayburn	Houston, TX
Goliad	Lone Star	Aquifer(s)	Annexation	Reconstruction
Oil	Comanche		Quanah Parker	Dallas
Constitution	San Antonio	Caddo	Sam Houston	Davy Crockett
Declaration of Independence	(Texas) Rangers	David G. Burnet	Jim Bowie	County(-ies)

Texas History Bingo

William Travis	Dallas	Lone Star	Guadelupe	Republic of Texas
Comanche	Alamo	Barbed Wire	Susanna Dickinson	Empresario(s)
Annexation	(Texas) Rangers		Reconstruction	Armadillo
Quanah Parker	Oil	Houston, TX	Constitution	Juneteenth
County(-ies)	Jim Bowie	David G. Burnet	Sam Houston	Juan Seguín

Texas History Bingo

Quanah Parker	Reconstruction	Houston, TX	Jim Bowie	Juan Seguín
Plains	Aquifer(s)	Susanna Dickinson	Sam Rayburn	Republic of Texas
Goodnight	Constitution		Tejanos	Texas Revolution
Dallas	President of the U.S.	(Texas) Rangers	David G. Burnet	Barbed Wire
El Paso	Declaration of Independence	Mirabeau B. Lamar	County(-ies)	Treaty of Guadalupe Hidalgo

Texas History Bingo

Declaration of Independence	**Tejanos**	**Annexation**	**Aquifer(s)**	**Jim Bowie**
Plains	**Dallas**	**Barbed Wire**	**Caddo**	**Alamo**
Rio Grande	**Treaty of Guadalupe Hidalgo**		**Cattle**	**Confederacy**
Davy Crockett	**Reconstruction**	**Flag(s)**	**Sam Houston**	**El Paso**
Lone Star	**David G. Burnet**	**President of the U.S.**	**Quanah Parker**	**Goodnight**

Texas History Bingo

Armadillo	Reconstruction	Juneteenth	Rio Grande	Treaty of Guadalupe Hidalgo
Guadelupe	Annexation	El Paso	Susanna Dickinson	Republic of Texas
Sam Rayburn	Barbed Wire		Aquifer(s)	Caddo
David G. Burnet	Houston, TX	Sam Houston	Mirabeau B. Lamar	Goodnight
Goliad	Dallas	Flag(s)	Juan Seguín	President of the U.S.

Texas History Bingo: Card No. 6

Texas History Bingo

Flag(s)	Caddo	Confederacy	Cattle	Lone Star
Goliad	Juan Seguín	Comanche	Alamo	Plains
Juneteenth	Texas Revolution		Reconstruction	Austin, TX
Quanah Parker	Constitution	Republic of Texas	William Travis	Oil
David G. Burnet	Jim Bowie	Sam Houston	Mirabeau B. Lamar	Armadillo

Texas History Bingo

Goodnight	Reconstruction	Borders	Guadelupe	Austin, TX
Plains	Rio Grande	Sam Rayburn	Treaty of Guadalupe Hidalgo	Aquifer(s)
Republic of Texas	Missions		Juan Seguín	Tejanos
County(-ies)	Quanah Parker	William Travis	El Paso	Constitution
(Texas) Rangers	David G. Burnet	Mirabeau B. Lamar	Annexation	Goliad

Texas History Bingo

Caddo	Lone Star	Comanche	Republic of Texas	Treaty of Guadalupe Hidalgo
El Paso	Rio Grande	Goodnight	Annexation	Juan Seguín
Empresario(s)	Flag(s)		Alamo	Borders
Austin, TX	Declaration of Independence	Houston, TX	Cattle	Confederacy
Constitution	Sam Houston	Barbed Wire	William Travis	Tejanos

Texas History Bingo: Card No. 9

Texas History Bingo

William Travis	Guadelupe	Aquifer(s)	Sam Rayburn	President of the U.S.
Treaty of Guadalupe Hidalgo	Austin, TX	Susanna Dickinson	Alamo	Juan Seguín
Missions	Reconstruction		Texas Revolution	Oil
Houston, TX	Davy Crockett	El Paso	Sam Houston	Empresario(s)
Stephen F. Austin	Goliad	Juneteenth	Declaration of Independence	Goodnight

Texas History Bingo

Armadillo	Reconstruction	El Paso	Annexation	Goliad
Borders	Empresario(s)	Cattle	Caddo	Susanna Dickinson
Plains	Rio Grande		Juneteenth	Comanche
Stephen F. Austin	Republic of Texas	Sam Houston	Jim Bowie	William Travis
Barbed Wire	David G. Burnet	Flag(s)	Mirabeau B. Lamar	Lone Star

Texas History Bingo

Lone Star	Tejanos	Empresario(s)	Guadelupe	Caddo
Comanche	(Texas) Rangers	Rio Grande	Mirabeau B. Lamar	Alamo
Flag(s)	Confederacy		Treaty of Guadalupe Hidalgo	Sam Rayburn
David G. Burnet	Constitution	Juan Seguín	William Travis	Plains
Reconstruction	Borders	Missions	Barbed Wire	Austin, TX

Texas History Bingo

Stephen F. Austin	Tejanos	Armadillo	Empresario(s)	Treaty of Guadalupe Hidalgo
Rio Grande	Borders	Reconstruction	Caddo	Oil
Guadelupe	Aquifer(s)		Comanche	Confederacy
Goodnight	Sam Houston	Austin, TX	Missions	William Travis
David G. Burnet	Davy Crockett	Mirabeau B. Lamar	Flag(s)	Cattle

Texas History Bingo

Jim Bowie	Rio Grande	Annexation	Sam Houston	Stephen F. Austin
Austin, TX	Flag(s)	Empresario(s)	Alamo	Reconstruction
El Paso	Texas Revolution		Juneteenth	Barbed Wire
Davy Crockett	Caddo	Missions	Aquifer(s)	Armadillo
David G. Burnet	Sam Rayburn	Oil	Goliad	Goodnight

Texas History Bingo

Cattle	Caddo	Annexation	Lone Star	Guadelupe
Armadillo	Juneteenth	Susanna Dickinson	Rio Grande	El Paso
Treaty of Guadalupe Hidalgo	Flag(s)		Republic of Texas	Juan Seguín
David G. Burnet	Empresario(s)	Borders	Sam Houston	Stephen F. Austin
Goliad	Constitution	Mirabeau B. Lamar	President of the U.S.	Comanche

Texas History Bingo

Aquifer(s)	Empresario(s)	Borders	President of the U.S.	San Antonio
Sam Rayburn	Oil	Confederacy	Plains	Texas Revolution
Stephen F. Austin	Tejanos		Treaty of Guadalupe Hidalgo	Comanche
Quanah Parker	Austin, TX	David G. Burnet	Cattle	William Travis
El Paso	Texas Independence Day	Mirabeau B. Lamar	Constitution	Reconstruction

Texas History Bingo

Stephen F. Austin	Sheep	Cotton	Empresario(s)	Jim Bowie
Cattle	El Paso	Sam Houston	Texas Revolution	Confederacy
Caddo	William Travis		Texas Independence Day	Borders
Declaration of Independence	Goliad	Goodnight	Annexation	Oil
Houston, TX	Barbed Wire	Lone Star	Guadelupe	Tejanos

Texas History Bingo

President of the U.S.	Missions	Austin, TX	El Paso	Sam Rayburn
Reconstruction	Stephen F. Austin	Houston, TX	Treaty of Guadalupe Hidalgo	Barbed Wire
Caddo	Oil		Cotton	Juan Seguín
Declaration of Independence	Susanna Dickinson	Sam Houston	William Travis	Juneteenth
Texas Independence Day	Empresario(s)	Annexation	Sheep	Armadillo

Texas History Bingo

Treaty of Guadalupe Hidalgo	Armadillo	Empresario(s)	Borders	Missions
Cattle	Guadelupe	Juan Seguín	Lone Star	Texas Revolution
Sheep	Jim Bowie		Alamo	President of the U.S.
Juneteenth	Texas Independence Day	Houston, TX	Constitution	Cotton
Republic of Texas	San Antonio	Goliad	Goodnight	Mirabeau B. Lamar

Texas History Bingo

Missions	Sheep	Guadelupe	Empresario(s)	Alamo
Aquifer(s)	Comanche	Plains	Houston, TX	Sam Rayburn
Tejanos	Confederacy		Quanah Parker	Susanna Dickinson
Declaration of Independence	Goodnight	County(-ies)	Constitution	Texas Independence Day
Dallas	(Texas) Rangers	San Antonio	William Travis	Cotton

Texas History Bingo

Cattle	Armadillo	Plains	Empresario(s)	Davy Crockett
Tejanos	Cotton	Austin, TX	Borders	Flag(s)
Oil	Goliad		Sheep	Annexation
Houston, TX	Lone Star	Texas Independence Day	Declaration of Independence	Goodnight
Quanah Parker	San Antonio	Mirabeau B. Lamar	Stephen F. Austin	Constitution

Texas History Bingo

Republic of Texas	Juneteenth	Cotton	Rio Grande	Stephen F. Austin
Sam Rayburn	Guadelupe	President of the U.S.	Borders	Alamo
Austin, TX	Texas Revolution		Flag(s)	Confederacy
Oil	Declaration of Independence	Constitution	Susanna Dickinson	Jim Bowie
San Antonio	Barbed Wire	Sheep	Texas Independence Day	Plains

Texas History Bingo

Aquifer(s)	Sheep	Lone Star	Rio Grande	Mirabeau B. Lamar
Armadillo	Missions	Goliad	Cattle	Susanna Dickinson
Juneteenth	Stephen F. Austin		County(-ies)	Flag(s)
San Antonio	Oil	Texas Independence Day	Barbed Wire	Constitution
Davy Crockett	Goodnight	(Texas) Rangers	Houston, TX	Cotton

Texas History Bingo

Aquifer(s)	Stephen F. Austin	Jim Bowie	Sheep	Borders
Treaty of Guadalupe Hidalgo	Mirabeau B. Lamar	Plains	Sam Rayburn	Flag(s)
Confederacy	President of the U.S.		Missions	Oil
Davy Crockett	County(-ies)	Texas Independence Day	Barbed Wire	Tejanos
Dallas	Quanah Parker	San Antonio	Guadelupe	(Texas) Rangers

Texas History Bingo

Quanah Parker	Plains	Sheep	Annexation	Cotton
Susanna Dickinson	Davy Crockett	Cattle	Aquifer(s)	Alamo
Tejanos	Borders		County(-ies)	Texas Independence Day
El Paso	Declaration of Independence	(Texas) Rangers	San Antonio	Texas Revolution
Mirabeau B. Lamar	Jim Bowie	Austin, TX	President of the U.S.	Dallas

Texas History Bingo

Cotton	Sheep	County(-ies)	Sam Rayburn	President of the U.S.
Houston, TX	Guadelupe	Borders	Missions	Aquifer(s)
Davy Crockett	Juneteenth		Texas Revolution	Quanah Parker
Stephen F. Austin	Rio Grande	Dallas	San Antonio	Texas Independence Day
Confederacy	El Paso	Annexation	(Texas) Rangers	Declaration of Independence

Texas History Bingo

County(-ies)	Austin, TX	Sheep	Missions	Comanche
Davy Crockett	Juneteenth	Cattle	Texas Independence Day	Alamo
Sam Houston	(Texas) Rangers		San Antonio	Quanah Parker
President of the U.S.	Armadillo	Plains	Dallas	Susanna Dickinson
Stephen F. Austin	Texas Revolution	Cotton	Republic of Texas	Confederacy

Texas History Bingo: Card No. 27

Texas History Bingo

Treaty of Guadalupe Hidalgo	Missions	William Travis	Sheep	Austin, TX
Comanche	Cotton	County(-ies)	Houston, TX	Texas Revolution
(Texas) Rangers	San Antonio		President of the U.S.	Sam Rayburn
Confederacy	Republic of Texas	Goliad	Oil	Texas Independence Day
Rio Grande	Caddo	Stephen F. Austin	Dallas	Davy Crockett

Texas History Bingo

Cotton	Missions	President of the U.S.	Cattle	Caddo
Davy Crockett	Houston, TX	Plains	Confederacy	Republic of Texas
Tejanos	County(-ies)		Declaration of Independence	Sheep
Comanche	Alamo	Juan Seguín	San Antonio	Texas Independence Day
Aquifer(s)	Borders	Dallas	Armadillo	(Texas) Rangers

Texas History Bingo

Jim Bowie	Sheep	Sam Rayburn	Caddo	Texas Independence Day
Susanna Dickinson	Juan Seguín	Juneteenth	Texas Revolution	Alamo
Dallas	Barbed Wire		Confederacy	Plains
Davy Crockett	Armadillo	Missions	San Antonio	County(-ies)
Declaration of Independence	Lone Star	(Texas) Rangers	Cotton	President of the U.S.